Presented to

_____

By

_____

Date

_____

BREATH
PRAYERS

or African Americans

Simple Whispers That Keep You in God's Presence

HONOR B BOOKS

Inspiration and Motivation for the Season of Life

COOK COMMUNICATIONS MINISTRIES
Colorado Springs, Colorado • Paris, Ontario
KINGSWAY COMMUNICATIONS LTD
Eastbourne, England

Honor Books® is an imprint of
Cook Communications Ministries, Colorado Springs, CO 80918
Cook Communications, Paris, Ontario
Kingsway Communications Ltd, Eastbourne, England

BREATH PRAYERS FOR AFRICAN AMERICANS—SIMPLE WHISPERS
THAT KEEP YOU IN GOD'S PRESENCE
© 2004 by BORDON BOOKS
6532 East 71st St, Suite 105
Tulsa, OK 74133

Printed in the United States of America.
   5 6 7 8 Printing/Year 08 07 06 05

Compiled and written by Edna G. Jordan
Cover designed by LJ Designs
Developed by Bordon Books

ISBN 1-56292-255-6

WHAT IS A BREATH PRAYER?

Even if you spend time in the morning with God, by the time you've finished item number ten on your list of things to do, the peace you felt may have evaporated; and perhaps He feels very far away. But He is as close as your breath; and you can spend your entire day with Him—even on the run. Breath prayers are brief, heartfelt prayers that can help you enjoy God's company and surround your loved ones with prayer without retreating to the mountains and giving up your to do list. The secret is a short prayer that you whisper to God as you go about the business of your day, allowing your experiences to prompt you. As you see a friend, you can pray, "Father, bless her." As you stand in line, you can pray "Father, bless her" for the cashier as someone argues with her. When you get to that three o'clock slump and wonder how you are going to get everything done, you can pray, "Father, bless me."

Instead of leaving God in the corner with your Bible, Breath prayers can help you to live a life in which God walks with you daily as you talk to Him about the things that cross your path. Your life will be transformed as you live continually in God's presence.

Best of all is it to preserve
everything in a pure, still heart,
and let there be for every
pulse a thanksgiving,
and for every breath a song.

KONRAD VON GESNER

Pray without ceasing.

1 THESSALONIANS 5:17 NKJV

How to Use
Breath Prayers for African Americans

After you have read **Breath Prayers for African Americans,** choose a suitable prayer to use throughout your day. Repeat it so that you can say it to yourself in one breath, both in and out. Each breath is a prayer. In this way you will pray without ceasing, aware of God walking through each experience with you.

As you see people or think of them, as you experience situations or feelings, offer that prayer to God. "I exalt You, Lord," can become the refrain of your heart when you see drivers around you on the road and as you see various other people in your daily life. "I exalt You, Lord," can mean you celebrate with God others' existence. It can mean you celebrate God's Lordship and loving care of them. It can also mean you praise God even though things are not going your way at the moment. The words will stay the same, but each breath you pray will be unique in the way you mean it to God. And you will maintain a constant connection with Him.

[Pray] always with all prayer and supplication in the Spirit, being watchful to this end with all perseverance and supplication for all the saints.

EPHESIANS 6:18 NKJV

I REST IN YOUR STRENGTH, LORD.

David was greatly distressed. . . . But David strengthened himself in the LORD his God.

1 SAMUEL 30:6 NASB

Someone once said, "When life gives you a lemon, just make lemonade."

That's a great way to face life's hurts and disappointments. Though it is not healthy to be pessimistic, it is wise to realize you can't change some things.

Even the best of well-ordered plans don't always work out.

It might be that when you have done your best, someone will find something wrong with it. Your good intentions could possibly be misunderstood. Or, you might sometimes find yourself facing unkind people—for whatever reason.

Though you care what others think, you cannot control what they think. So, how do you handle these things?

Rest in God's strength just as David did. God will overshadow you with His love, His mercy, and His encouragement.

Begin by reading what His Word says about you.

I can pray the breath prayer, *I rest in Your strength, Lord,* when—

- someone laughs at my mistakes.

- I feel like a failure.

- I am embarrassed.

- I feel insignificant.

- others do not have confidence in me.

- I am afraid to try again.

- I feel unattractive.

  I rest in Your strength, Lord.

FILL ME WITH YOUR JOY, FATHER.

I have loved you, [just] as the Father has loved Me. . . . I have told you these things, that My joy and delight may be in you, and that your joy and gladness may be full.

JOHN 15:9,11 AMP

Trouble and sorrow continually plague mankind. God knew you couldn't escape them, so He provided His joy for you. He placed it in your heart so it's accessible any time and any place.

When you find yourself feeling down, or things are just not going right, pray a breath prayer for God's joy to rise up in you. It will flow from your heart into praise and worship unto Him.

His joy strengthens you so you don't feel

sorry for yourself. You smile when others are discourteous or impatient. You're happy for those who tell you of their good fortune.

But God's joy is not just for you. God wants you to share it with others. It will make the day brighter for everyone.

I can pray the breath prayer, *Fill me with Your joy, Father,* when—

- I'm sad or depressed.

- I'm lonely.

- I feel irritable.

- I feel weak.

- I'm faced with unpleasant people.

- I have an unpleasant job to do.

- I need to encourage others.

Fill me with Your joy, Father.

MAY MY WORDS REFLECT YOUR TRUTH.

*Each of you must put off falsehood
and speak truthfully.*

EPHESIANS 4:25 NIV

Lies can easily be excused or justified and the blame put on someone else.

You may be guilty of having made statements such as these: "It's not my fault." "She should have paid attention." "Anyway, they owe me." "He won't miss it." "I'll pay you back." "It's only a penny." "No one saw me." "I didn't mean it." "You misunderstood." "I'll have it next week."

God's Word is truth. It's impossible for Him to lie. Jesus said that He is the truth and that the truth will set you free. You have such confidence in His truthfulness that you placed your life in His hands. You trust Him to do what He says. You are His child and the new nature He has put in you makes you just like Him in this regard. Lies are part of the old life, and in His love and power you can leave them behind.

Pray a breath prayer to Him to help you speak and do whatever is truthful—regardless of the situation or the circumstances.

You please Him when you make yourself accountable and responsible to live honestly—in word and deed.

Don't add to or take from the truth, but keep it real.

I can pray the breath prayer, *May my words reflect Your truth,* when—

- I conduct business.

- I apply for a job.

- I am asked to be a witness.

- I recount a story.

- I prepare my taxes.

- I do anything.

May my words reflect Your truth.

MAY I LOVE LIKE YOU, JESUS.

*May the Lord make you
increase and abound in love
to one another and to all.*

1 THESSALONIANS 3:12 NKJV

The world has many meanings for the word love. But so often they can leave people confused, hurt, and bitter.

The love the Bible speaks about is not like that. The Bible says God is love. He loves you so much that He sent His only Son to die for you. That's how precious you are to Him. You did nothing to deserve His love or to earn it. God loves you unconditionally.

You have a place in His heart that He set aside just for you. You don't have to compete with others for His attention. No one can return that love to Him in the special way you do.

And God has placed His love in you for the purpose of reaching out to others so that they accept and trust His love for them.

Pray a breath prayer that you will love others with the kind of love that God has for you and them.

I can pray the breath prayer, *May I love like You, Jesus,* when—

- I am mistreated.

- I am misunderstood.

- others are quarreling.

- others feel that no one cares.

- others are not deserving of my love.

- I don't feel as if I can.

May I love like You, Jesus.

GIVE ME A PURE HEART, FATHER.

Who may stand in his holy place?
Only those whose hands and hearts are pure.

PSALM 24:3-4 NLT

Impurity has many faces and many disguises. Sometimes it flaunts itself and at other times it's hidden—suggestive and subtle. We are bombarded with it in the media every day. Some erroneously think it applies only to sexual conduct. While it appears that is the predominant influence, it is not the only one.

And it all begins in the heart. Is your heart completely loyal to God? Do you love Him more than you love what the world offers, more than temptations that call to you in stores, on television, at work? James said that pure religion is to love the helpless and to keep yourself unstained by the world. All day long you make choices and decisions that express the condition of your heart.

16

As God's child, open your heart to Him. Pray a breath prayer inviting Him to help you examine your motives, thoughts, and feelings. Be sensitive to His instruction and correction. And have confidence that, as you pray, He will change your desires and strengthen your will to do what pleases Him.

God knows your sincere desire is to please Him. Your prayer invites Him to create His purity in you.

I can pray the breath prayer, *Give me a pure heart, Father,* when—

- I make choices and decisions.

- I am tempted.

- I see others accept impurity.

- I am alone.

- I enjoy entertainment.

- I perform daily activities.

   Give me a pure heart, Father.

REVEAL YOUR WISE WAYS, GOD.

Wisdom has the advantage of giving success.

ECCLESIASTES 10:10 NASB

On the first day of your new job you discover that you are the only minority in the department. Everyone is kind and friendly, but they seem awkward as they try to make you feel welcome. What can you say or do to ease the tension?

Your five-year-old daughter's feelings are hurt because her dark, curly hair is different than the straight blonde hair of her classmates. How do you make her understand and appreciate her unique beauty?

As you leave a popular designer boutique, you chat with two neighbors who have just arrived. After your good-byes, you remember you left your car keys in the dressing room. Quietly you enter the dressing room, only to overhear the same two neighbors whispering about you. How could you, a receptionist, possibly afford to shop at such an elaborate boutique, they wonder.

Do you wait to confront them? Or do you choose to pity their prejudice and quietly leave?

God's wisdom is your answer. It will show you what to say and do so you can successfully handle any situation.

I can pray the breath prayer, *Reveal Your wise ways, God,* when—

- I don't know the reasons why.

- I must answer a difficult question.

- someone asks me for advice.

- things do not happen as I planned.

- I must solve a problem.

- I face unpleasant situations.

- I must make an important decision.

Reveal Your wise ways, God.

I HUMBLE MYSELF, LORD.

Humble yourselves before the Lord,
and he will lift you up.

JAMES 4:10 NIV

We all have someone in our lives whom we admire and want to please. We do whatever is necessary to get their attention or to earn their favor. Sometimes, we mistakenly base our worth on their opinion of us. Yet no one esteems you as highly as God does. He has given you dignity. He favors you and He gives you favor with others.

It's easy to become proud when you are complimented. It's easy to take credit for an accomplishment and pat yourself on the back, forgetting all the talents and opportunities with which God has provided you. Pray a breath prayer for God's help to remain humble so you will remember that you did not do these things on your own. God made them possible because He loves you.

Christ humbled himself and did not seek glory that belonged to God. He did it for you, and God exalted Him for it at the proper time. In a similar way, God will exalt you in His perfect timing as you humble yourself and give credit where credit is due—to God.

I can pray the breath prayer, *I humble myself, Lord,* when—

- I am promoted.

- I pray.

- I am chastised.

- I want to defend myself.

- You give me my desires.

- others compliment me.

- important people favor and befriend me.

I humble myself, Lord.

I NEED BOLDNESS, ALMIGHTY GOD.

*I have great boldness and free
and fearless confidence.*

2 CORINTHIANS 7:4 AMP

Injustice. Harassment. Accusations. Bullying. Abuse. Oppression.

Most likely you will experience or witness some of these mistreatments in this life—whether in school, at work, in public, or maybe even in your own home. But rest assured that God is not responsible for any of them because He is love.

David was a young man who understood God's power, God's purposes, and God's love for His people. This is what empowered him to boldly step forward and slay Goliath, the giant who insulted and taunted the Israelite army.

Spend time getting to know God. Learn to know what He thinks about the situations in your life. Be sure your attitude and your behavior are proper. Understand what God wants you to do or not to do. Do not confuse boldness with loudness. Trust God to take care of you and handle the situation.

I can pray the breath prayer, *I need boldness, Almighty God,* when—

- I am called to be a witness.

- I have to speak in front of others.

- I have to ask a question.

- someone insults You.

- I am chosen to be in charge.

- I have to speak out against wrong.

- I request what is rightfully mine.

I need boldness, Almighty God.

GIVE ME PATIENCE, LORD.

You . . . must be patient.

JAMES 5:8 NLT

How often do you glance at your watch during a church service? Is it hard to resist rushing across the railroad tracks to beat a slow-moving train? Are you short with the cashier who has to verify the sale price of an item? Do you interrupt someone to make your point just so you will not forget it? Patience is the focus of these real-life situations.

With all the technological conveniences in the world today, you can become so accustomed to convenience that you expect it everywhere you go and in everything you do.

Remember how God created everything? Everything occurred on the appropriate day, in the right order. In the end, He "saw that all of it was good." Consider how patiently God waited for you to receive Him. You were well worth the wait. God's perfect timing was at work in your life. Patience is a virtue that recognizes God's timetable.

I can pray the breath prayer, *Give me patience, Lord*, when—

- I have to wait in traffic.

- I have to wait in a checkout line.

- others are talking.

- I am teaching or training someone.

- I am given an assignment with many steps to follow.

- I am behind someone in line who is elderly or needs assistance.

- I am waiting to hear from You.

Give me patience, Lord.

LIFT MY HEART WITH LAUGHTER, FATHER.

There is a time for everything,
and a season for every activity under heaven:
. . . A time to weep and a time to laugh.

ECCLESIASTES 3:1,4 NIV

You've heard, I'm sure, that it takes more facial muscles to frown than to smile. Is it possible that laughter can actually help the healing process as some say? Proverbs 17:22 AMP says, "A happy heart is good medicine and a cheerful mind works healing."

When you are tempted to dwell on something sad or painful, ask God to help you remember something uplifting and cheerful—even humorous —and think about that.

Learn to be a good sport and let others

know it's okay to play an innocent joke on you. Don't allow your race to be an excuse for touchiness. And learn to laugh at yourself. That's a great pick-me-up. You can also watch a wholesome, funny movie or read a lighthearted novel. Maybe you have a friend whose silly antics you cannot help but laugh at.

Life will always have its serious moments, but thank God for times when you can let down your guard and have a good laugh.

I can pray the breath prayer, *Lift my heart with laughter, Father,* when—

- I feel low.

- something I value is accidentally broken.

- I feel annoyed or irritable.

- things do not happen as I hoped.

- others refuse to be happy.

- others see my mistakes.

Lift my heart with laughter, Father.

GIVE ME A HEART OF COURAGE, LORD.

The Lord is with me;
I will not be afraid.

PSALM 118:6 NIV

Fear is a paralyzing and deadly foe. It can hinder you from making decisions. It can stop you from fulfilling your dreams, destroy relationships, steal your peace, and even kill. Luke 21:26 NKJV says people's hearts will fail because of fear.

Almighty God does not want you to be afraid. In fact, He has told you not to fear. Because He told you that, He will provide what you need in order for you not to fear. God's very presence is His greatest provision. He is greater and mightier in you than he who is in the world

(1 John 4:4 AMP). He is also a protective shield around you (Psalm 3:3 NLT).

As you place your trust in God, you will find courage to face life's challenges. As you rest in Him and recognize that He is there for you at every turn, your faith will grow and dispel fear.

I can pray the breath prayer, *Give me a heart of courage, Lord,* when—

- I face the unfamiliar or the unknown.

- I have to stand up for what is right.

- I face prejudice.

- I am threatened.

- I am in scary places.

- no one is around to help me.

   Give me a heart of courage, Lord.

PUT A SONG IN MY HEART, GOD.

Sing to the Lord a new song.

PSALM 149:1 NLT

Is there anything as moving as your favorite song? Gospel. Classical. Rap. Rhythm and blues. Rock and roll. Country and western. Soul. Opera. Musicals. Lullabies.

Songs are sung to babies in the womb and when they are being rocked to sleep. Nursery rhymes and childhood games are frequently put to music. Songs are sung during courtship and marriage. Songs celebrate and lift one's spirit.

The Bible speaks of the importance of singing praise to God. In the Old Testament, musicians and singers sometimes went out in front of the Israelite armies, and battles were won without even one sword being drawn. The book of Isaiah says the mountains and trees sing to God.

Even if you are not in the choir, you can sing your own praise to God for His goodness. It does not matter if you can't carry a tune as long as your heart is in tune with Him.

I can pray the breath prayer, *Put a song in my heart, God*, when—

- I feel happy.

- I feel sad.

- I feel like giving up.

- I am tempted to forget Your goodness to me.

- everything seems to go wrong.

- good things happen to others.

Put a song in my heart, God.

MAY I SPEAK ONLY YOUR WORDS, FATHER.

The tongue is a small thing, but what enormous damage it can do.

JAMES 3:5 NLT

Does the slightest annoyance cause you to grumble and criticize? Are you quick to give someone a piece of your mind? Is it hard for you to keep a confidence? Do you quickly label someone as being prejudiced just because they do not agree with your opinions or side with you? Do you gravitate toward those who gossip?

We all struggle with the impulse to speak when keeping silent is the wiser thing to do. Often the more we trust God to work things out in His own way and His own time, the less we feel we have to say something in our defense.

When God spoke, whatever He said came to pass. He created you in His image, and your words also have power to hurt or help. Use your words for good. God will help you say the right thing, in the right way, at the right time, in the right place, and to the right person.

He will also show you when to still your voice and trust Him to work in His own way.

I can pray the breath prayer, *May I speak only Your words, Father,* when—

- I am hurt or angry.

- I am tempted to criticize or complain.

- I want to slander or gossip.

- others are determined to argue.

- someone else is talking.

- I am not sure I am right about something.

May I speak only Your words, Father.

BE MY GOD OF ALL COMFORT, FATHER OF MERCIES.

*Let . . . Your merciful kindness
and steadfast love be for my comfort,
according to Your promise.*

PSALM 119:76 AMP

The world offers many pseudo-comforts for whatever ails you. Some eat food as a comfort for loneliness. Others find comfort in extramarital affairs because of problems they don't care to deal with. Teenagers join gangs to fulfill a desire to belong. Alcohol is a comfort for some who want to forget their hurts and failures. Some take drugs to escape boredom, and some bully or abuse others in an attempt to cover their emotional insecurities and downtrodden self-esteem.

Almighty God has such love and compassion

for you that He sent His Son to die for you. Jesus Christ is your High Priest. He understands your weaknesses because He has faced all the temptations you face (Hebrews 4:15 NLT). And He is the God of all comfort and Father of mercies (2 Corinthians 1:3 NASB).

When you need a shoulder to cry on, God has given you access to His throne. You can rest assured that there will not be any regrets when you go to Him for comfort.

I can pray the breath prayer, *Be my God of all comfort, Father of mercies*, when—

- I feel lonely.

- I feel no one understands or cares.

- no one has time to talk to me.

- I feel sorry for myself.

- I am worried and afraid.

- I feel physical pain.

Be my God of all comfort, Father of mercies.

Watch over us all, Father.

Pray for each other.

James 5:16 niv

Have you ever been busy and had a friend's face briefly cross your mind? Maybe you are in a business meeting when you think of a relative you have not seen in years. Perhaps you are enjoying a movie with your family, when suddenly you seem to hear a church member's name in your heart.

For whatever reason, consider the person's name or face a prompting from God to pray. While everything may be going well with you, it might not be so great for someone else. And even if you are going through a rough time, someone just might be having a harder time than you. It could appear as though everything is fine in their life. Pray anyway.

What a wonderful thing it is that God has entrusted that person into your hands. Just as He brings someone to your attention, He will place your face or name in someone else's heart and mind when you are in need of prayer.

I can pray the breath prayer, *Watch over us all, Father,* when—

- their face or name crosses my mind.

- they are in trouble or have a need.

- my path crosses theirs today.

- they are too burdened to pray for themselves.

- they do not know how to pray for themselves.

- they have treated me wrong.

Watch over us all, Father.

HELP ME BE CREATIVE, LORD.

*God gave them knowledge and skill
in all learning and wisdom.*

DANIEL 1:17 AMP

Think about the excitement you experience with something new. You can hardly wait to show off your latest hairstyle or that new outfit. You lie awake planning how to succeed on your new job. Maybe you have begun decorating your new home.

Eventually, the new becomes familiar and rather comfortable, and after a while it even becomes old. In a way, that is good because no one could endure a new adrenaline rush every day—all day long.

On the other hand, you must not allow boredom to subtly creep in when things become ordinary, familiar, and old. God does not want you to be bored because that would hinder you from enjoying the wonderful life He has for you.

Romans 6:4 NIV says that God wants you to live a new life. So, if you feel that each day brings the "same ol', same ol'," ask God for fresh, new ideas.

Take some refresher courses. Find a new hobby. Give yourself a new look. 2 Corinthians 5:17 NIV says that the new has come!

I can pray the breath prayer, *Help me be creative, Lord,* when—

- I feel bored with everything being the same.

- I face a perplexing problem.

- I want to find a different way to do my job.

- I want to decorate or remodel my home.

- I am part of a committee.

- I cook a meal.

- I brainstorm at a business meeting.

Help me be creative, Lord.

LORD, I GIVE YOU THANKS.

Always give thanks for everything to God the Father in the name of our Lord Jesus Christ.

EPHESIANS 5:20 NLT

"Thank you" are two very simple, yet profound, words. From the heart, they convey humble appreciation for someone's kindness. But sometimes kindness is taken for granted.

Do you feel that because something is owed you, saying thank you is not necessary? Be thankful when a favor or gift is large or small, whether it comes from the company president or a coworker. Say thank you when you are at home and also in public.

Think about your Heavenly Father's love. Learn to thank Him for who He is instead of asking for something all the time. Be thankful when He answers your prayer, and especially thank Him when He gives you that secret desire of your heart—the one that you never really prayed for. Be thankful when life is good, and thank Him for His faithfulness when you are in trouble.

Ask God to help you remember to be thankful—no matter what. Do not become presumptuous and take God's goodness or others' kindness for granted. Say thank you for every good thing that comes from God (James 1:17 NIV). And if you do, you will find that you'll experience a fundamental change of heart. You will feel happy and loved by God.

I can pray the breath prayer, *Lord, I give You thanks,* when—

- a favor or gift is large or small.
- I feel dissatisfied.
- I see others' misfortune.
- I see others' dreams fulfilled.
- You answer my prayers and when I'm waiting.
- life is good or not so good.

Lord, I give You thanks.

I BELIEVE I WILL SEE YOUR GOODNESS, LORD.

*I am still confident of this: I will see
the goodness of the Lord.*

PSALM 27:13 NIV

Life's situations are not always good and neither are people's attitudes or behavior. When bad things continually happen, discouragement and possibly pessimism are quick to knock on your door.

God does not want you to allow the hardships of life to distort or dim your outlook. He does not want you to conclude that everyone is rotten through and through just because you have been mistreated more times than you care to remember.

He is always there for you, and He has

promised to cause all things to work together for good because you love Him (Romans 8:28). He also promised that you would be satisfied with His goodness (Jeremiah 31:14).

So, in spite of negative situations and contrary people, believe that God will show you His goodness, for He will.

I can pray the breath prayer, *I believe I will see Your goodness, Lord,* when—

- things look really bad.

- things seem to get worse.

- others see only the bad.

- I did all I could to help.

- it seems that my prayers did no good.

I believe I will see Your goodness, Lord.

MAY I BE A FRIEND LIKE YOU, JESUS.

A friend is always loyal.
PROVERBS 17:17 NLT

The friendship between Jonathan, King Saul's son, and David was incredible (1 Samuel 19-20). Their love and loyalty to each other is an example for every Christian to follow.

True friendship cannot be based on looks, possessions, or titles. The inner qualities of character and personality are more important.

Friends are truthful and honorable. They are selfless, have each other's best interest at heart, and do not abuse the relationship. Friends are trustworthy, dependable, and loyal. They are loving, kind, and quick to forgive. Proverbs 18:24 mentions a friend who sticks closer than a brother. Christ Jesus is that friend. Like Jesus, a true friend loves you despite your faults and sees you as God sees you.

I can pray the breath prayer, *May I be a friend like You, Jesus,* when—

- someone needs a shoulder to cry on.

- someone needs encouragement.

- someone needs a favor.

- someone cannot return the favor.

- someone feels alone.

- someone is hurting.

- someone is afraid.

May I be a friend like You, Jesus.

I ENTRUST MY WAY TO YOU, SOVEREIGN GOD.

Do not fret . . .
Commit your way to the LORD, trust
also in Him, and He will do it.

PSALM 37:1,5 NASB

You have opportunities every day to fret—to become worried, annoyed, disturbed, irritated, vexed, or just plain worn out by the pressures of life. Technology, which is supposed to make life easier and more productive, can actually cause pressure. You push yourself to do more in less time. And you try to cram more activities into the extra time you manage to save.

And sometimes people cause pressure: impatient drivers, slow waiters, rude cashiers, discourteous shoppers, even intruding telemarketers. Slow service in a restaurant or waiting for a doctor appointment can be annoying.

Situations like these can cause you to fret, but God said not to. Fretting only makes things worse. Say a breath prayer and rely on God's faithfulness to take care of things you cannot do anything about.

I can pray the breath prayer, *I entrust my way to You, Sovereign God*, when—

- I am on time but others are not.

- others are slow.

- others are impatient with me.

- I am at a standstill in traffic or I have to wait in a long checkout line.

- I want to control what is only in Your power.

- I am given an assignment at the last minute.

- there is an incorrect charge on my bill.

I entrust my way to You, Sovereign God.

I TRUST YOU FOR THE FUTURE, LORD.

"I know the plans I have for you,"
declares the Lord, "plans to prosper you . . .
to give you hope and a future."

JEREMIAH 29:11 NIV

There is security in working for the same company for a considerable length of time. Everything is going along just fine, so why change anything? As the saying goes, "If it's not broke, then don't fix it!"

But, on the other hand, you can feel a false sense of security. You might become so settled and comfortable that you do not prepare for the possibility of *"what if . . . ?"*

The future can be good or bad—depending on in whom you put your trust. With the sincerest of hearts and best of intentions, people can still fail you. Situations are unstable because they can change. Put your trust in the One who does not change (Malachi 3:6).

God is your partner and all things work together for your good—fitting into a plan if you love the Lord. Almighty God has your future already planned and prepared—and it is good.

I can pray the breath prayer, *I trust You for the future, Lord,* when—

- the company I work for is downsizing.

- I face financial difficulties.

- I am fatigued from studying for school exams.

- the economy is rumored to be floundering.

- others are fearful of the future.

I trust You for the future, Lord.

BE WITH ME, FATHER.

*"Do not be afraid or discouraged,
for the Lord . . . will be with you; he will
neither fail you nor forsake you."*

DEUTERONOMY 31:8 NLT

Have you ever seen a movie where the most terrifying bully is made to look like a defeated coward? His friends may have run off and left him defenseless, standing alone in shameful defeat. The hero, fighting for a righteous cause, squares his shoulders and lifts his head as he makes a valiant stand alone.

Isn't it ironic that both are alone, but their demeanors are totally opposite? The bully, who originally had the upper hand, is afraid because he no longer has the support of others to help build his confidence. The suffering hero is brave and doesn't need others to buoy his confidence.

How do you feel when you take a stand for what is right? Do you need a cheering crowd to boost your courage? Or do you rely on your Heavenly Father for the approval and support you need?

Ask Him to let His presence be known. Trust Him—He is there.

I can pray the breath prayer, *Be with me, Father,* when—

- I am called to be a witness.

- I speak what You tell me.

- I do what You tell me.

- others turn their backs against me.

- others make fun of me.

- I have made a mistake.

Be with me, Father.

GOD OF WISDOM, HELP ME THINK CLEARLY.

*God . . . has given us a . . . calm
and well-balanced mind..*

2 TIMOTHY 1:7 AMP

You have so much to do and so little time—errands to run, job projects, meetings, social functions, appointments, family obligations, church, calls to make. Where does it end? You might have so much to do that you feel ready to go crazy.

You are pulled in so many directions that you are not finishing one thing before you begin another. Stop. Ask God to help you establish priorities—beginning with your relationship with Him. The success of everything else depends on that.

Acknowledge that you have limitations. Realize that there is an appropriate time to say a courteous but firm no without feeling guilty.

Thinking clearly will help you rearrange your hectic schedule. God desires that you live a well-balanced life. He will show you what is good for you and He will help you handle it.

I can pray the breath prayer, *God of Wisdom, help me think clearly,* when—

- I am driving.

- I am given an opportunity.

- I am given an ultimatum.

- I must give an explanation.

- I must make a decision.

- my children need my time.

- I carry out my daily activities.

- I balance my checkbook.

- I am given a job or assignment.

God of Wisdom, help me think clearly.

MAKE ME MORE LIKE YOU, FATHER.

*We are no longer to be children, . . .
carried about by every wind of doctrine,
by the trickery of men . . . but . . . we are to
grow up in all aspects into Him.*

EPHESIANS 4:14-15 NASB

"Why don't you grow up?" "You're such a
baby!" "You're just not ready for this!"

Has anyone ever made these statements to
you? Were they right, at the time? Have you
matured since then?

When you were a baby, your parents were
ecstatic over every new thing you did. Each
attempt and accomplishment was celebrated
because it proved that you were healthy and
growing. Each year, your physical and mental
growth was closely monitored to make sure you
were developing as expected. Perhaps if there

was the slightest hint of a shortcoming, parents, grandparents, teachers, guidance counselors, and church members rallied to help you overcome them.

Your Heavenly Father has a greater concern. He desires that you mature spiritually. John 6:63 says that His words are spirit and life. Study your Bible so that you grow up healthy and strong in your spirit. God is pleased as you become more like Him.

I can pray the breath prayer, *Make me more like You, Father,* when—

- I study Your Word.

- I obey Your Word.

- I pray.

- I face life's situations.

- I follow Christian leadership.

- I am given responsibility in my church.

Make me more like You, Father.

HEAL MY BROKEN HEART, JESUS.

*The Lord . . . has sent me to bind up
and heal the brokenhearted.*

ISAIAH 61:1 AMP

Psalm 119:68 says your Heavenly Father is good and He does what is good. Unfortunately, life is not always good, and neither are people. The proverbial "got up on the wrong side of the bed" sometimes results in cutting remarks and unkind behavior that really hurt. And sometimes it seems that everyone is "having a bad day!"

Perhaps your marital rights have been violated. Or you have had enough of turning the other cheek to a domineering supervisor. Maybe a trusted friend betrayed your confidence, or it was the unfriendly neighbor who scowled at your friendly smile and pleasant "Good morning!"

It has been said that physical wounds seem to heal more quickly than emotional ones. Christ Jesus was no stranger to hurts and pain. He is your High Priest who understands and sympathizes (Hebrews 4:15 AMP). Open your heart to Him and let Him work a healing miracle.

I can pray the breath prayer, *Heal my broken heart, Jesus,* when—

- my friends let me down.

- my marriage falls apart.

- other Christians do not show the love of God.

- my kindness is not returned.

- I am treated unfairly.

- my trust is betrayed.

- I am slandered.

Heal my broken heart, Jesus.

LORD, HELP ME REALIZE THAT I CAN'T DO IT WITHOUT YOU.

I can do everything with the help of Christ who gives me the strength I need.

PHILIPPIANS 4:13 NLT

There is a certain feeling of pride in accomplishing something yourself. Do you remember how you felt when you first learned to put your shoes on the right feet and then laced them correctly? And what about how good it felt the first time your parents let you drive the car alone?

When you are learning something new, you appreciate and welcome instruction and assistance. But once you get the hang of it, you have proven yourself capable of handling it.

Your relationship with God is different. Yes, He is pleased with your maturity, but any thought that you do not need His help is deceptive. We all live, move, and exist in Him (Acts 17:28 NLT). Apart from Him, we can do nothing (John 15:5 NLT). In addition, a project you can do by yourself can become something quite wonderful if you are willing to be guided by the God who is all-wise and all-knowing.

Even in the simplest job or responsibility, acknowledge your need of Him.

I can pray the breath prayer, *Lord, help me realize that I can't do it without You,* when—

- I do the same job.
- I feel confident and secure.
- I have to learn a new job.
- I take on a special project.
- the job is complicated.
- I handle my daily affairs.
- I work alone.
- I work with others.

Lord, help me realize that I can't do it without You.

GIVE ME A HEART OF REPENTANCE, SAVIOR.

If you . . . remember a grudge a friend has against you, . . . immediately, go to this friend and make things right. Then and only then, come back and work things out with God.

MATTHEW 5:23-24 MSG

It is easy to become so wrapped up in our personal lives that we feel independent—almost unaware of others. Often, we unintentionally say or do what we feel is right for ourselves without regard for the feelings of others.

It is hard for most of us to admit when we are wrong. Asking someone's forgiveness is even harder, but God requires it. Maybe it is His way of teaching us humility. Could it be that He is helping us get rid of pride and selfishness?

We must realize that although each of us is different, our lives touch and our paths cross in some way. And only God is right about everything all the time. The rest of us are capable of making mistakes.

Be humble enough to admit you're wrong and ask forgiveness of your Heavenly Father and others.

I can pray the breath prayer, *Give me a heart of repentance, Savior,* when—

- I disobey You.

- I hurt someone's feelings.

- I am discourteous.

- I cause trouble for others.

- I speak or act too quickly.

- I do not keep my word.

Give me a heart of repentance, Savior.

GOD, RELEASE ME FROM MY PAST.

I am still not all I should be, but I am focusing all my energies on this one thing: Forgetting the past and looking forward to what lies ahead.

PHILIPPIANS 3:13 NLT

Have you ever known someone who consistently talked about what they used to be, used to do, or how they used to look or live? Perhaps it seemed that they never had anything to look forward to.

God does not want you to dwell on your past and miss out on enjoying the wonderful future He has for you. Remember what happened to Lot's wife when she looked back at Sodom and Gomorrah after God's angel helped them flee from that wicked place (Genesis 19)?

And, even if you feel that your past was not

so bad, still you were a sinner—alienated from God until Christ Jesus saved you and made you God's child.

So, whether your past was so awful that you do not care to think about it or it seemed better than what you have now, God has something better for you. Don't look back and miss all He has laid out before you.

I can pray the breath prayer, *God, release me from my past,* when—

- a longtime friend brings up "the good old days."

- my future seems uncertain.

- I am tempted to remember my past mistakes.

- I return home to visit family and friends.

- I am disappointed with my present life.

- I feel a loss for what used to be.

    Lord, release me from my past.

LORD, TEACH ME WHAT TO SAY.

My tongue is the pen of a skillful writer.

PSALM 45:1 NIV

Have you ever been unsure of what to say? Perhaps you were embarrassed because you spoke too quickly and "put your foot in your mouth." Or, maybe you did not speak up quickly enough and someone else was given something that you really desired.

Some people seem to have a natural "gift of gab" while others have to take courses in public speaking. Some people can say a lot with a few words, while others ramble on and on and say nothing.

Skill is necessary in order to say the right thing—whether you are giving an eloquent speech at a banquet or giving your dog a command.

Your Heavenly Father knows the importance of saying the right words because that is how He created this world. And He is ready to help you say the right thing, whether you are worshipping and praying to Him or talking to others.

I can pray the breath prayer, *Lord, teach me what to say,* when—

- I am falsely accused.

- I chair a meeting.

- I make a toast.

- I admonish my child.

- I am complimented.

- I must decline an offer.

- I must apologize.

Lord, teach me what to say.

BE MY GOOD SHEPHERD WHO NEVER LOSES ME.

*The words he had spoken
would be fulfilled: "I have not lost
one of those you gave me."*

JOHN 18:9 NIV

Many of us remember the hiding games we played with our parents. They covered their eyes and counted while we hurriedly found the perfect hiding place. Many times we hid in a conspicuous place because we really wanted to be found. We covered our mouths to stifle our giggles while they searched for us and called our name.

Suddenly, their smiling faces appeared and we squealed with delight as they brought us out into the light and into their loving arms. Being found was more fun than hiding!

When you were not a Christian, it was as if you were in darkness and could not see your way. Do you remember the comforting love of God when He called your name? What joy you felt when you looked into the brightness of His smiling face!

Remember that love and joy when you feel you have messed up so badly that you have lost your way again. Run to His outstretched arms. The Good Shepherd does not lose His sheep!

I can pray the breath prayer, *Be my Good Shepherd who never loses me,* when—

- I do not know which way to go.

- I do not have clear direction.

- I feel lonely.

- I do not feel Your presence.

- I feel that I am at a standstill.

- I feel that others have left me behind.

Be my Good Shepherd who never loses me.

I TRUST YOU, LORD.

*I have put my trust in the Lord God
and made Him my refuge.*

PSALM 73:28 AMP

We live in a time when it seems the most stalwart things—from people to corporations to governments—seem a bit shaky. Winds of change have caused upheaval and unrest. Security has been breached in areas we never thought possible. And rumblings of fear can be heard in our land. We have found that our judicial system has cracks, and what we have built on it is tottering. The stock market proves that there is no permanent stability in financial or material wealth. We never imagined that we would see long-standing businesses and corporations downsizing or closing.

What we unconsciously deemed as indestructible now seems vulnerable. We sadly concede that those whom we have most admired and honored have flaws and are prone to error. Do you suppose this is why God says we are not to trust riches, or ourselves, or humankind?

God's eyes watch over you and He does not want you to fret or lose sleep over these things. Put your trust in Him and He will give you perfect peace and keep you safe.

I can pray the breath prayer, *I trust You, Lord,* when—

- I feel unsafe.

- others are afraid.

- I am alone.

- I am threatened.

- I read or hear bad news.

- I am away from my children or family.

I trust You, Lord.

FATHER, YOU ARE THE ONE WHO LIFTS UP MY HEAD.

*O Lord; you bestow glory on me
and lift up my head.*

PSALM 3:3 NIV

Before you became a child of God, you probably bowed to many troubles, sorrows, and heavy burdens. Perhaps the condemnation and guilt from your wrongdoing pressed you down even lower. No doubt while your head was bowed, you hid your face in your hands and cried many tears of shame and defeat. Unconsciously, you acknowledged that all those hardships had the power to bring you down and make you submit.

There are still some rough spots now that

you are His child. The difference is that you willingly bow in reverence and love to Him as He invites you to cast all your care over on Him (1 Peter 5:7). He has promised to make you shine. You know that you can trust Him because He is faithful. Now, you can cry tears of joy as He lifts up your head so that you look into His sweet loving face. You are restored completely.

I can pray the breath prayer, *Father, You are the One who lifts up my head,* when—

- I feel ashamed because I made a mistake.

- others say I am a failure.

- I feel burdened.

- I have lost hope.

- I feel low self-esteem.

- I need courage.

Father, You are the One who lifts up my head.

LORD, HAVE MERCY ON ME!

Bless the Lord . . . Who . . .
crowns you with loving-kindness
and tender mercy.

PSALM 103:2,4 AMP

Aren't you relieved when you make a mistake and someone says, "Don't worry about it"? Or have you ever had a late fee waived on your account? Maybe someone paid for your lunch when you were short on money.

Most likely you are very grateful when kindnesses such as these are freely shown to you. Though you were responsible for these things, others sympathized and stood in the gap for you. They forgave you, cancelled charges, and paid your debt.

Doesn't that sound just like God's love and mercy to you? Thank God that His mercies are new every morning, because every day there is a possibility that you will fall short or not do the right thing.

I can pray the breath prayer, *Lord, have mercy on me!* when—

- I don't hear You speaking to my heart.

- I make mistakes.

- I do foolish things.

- my mistakes cause problems for others.

- I speak or act before I think.

- others refuse to show me mercy.

Lord, have mercy on me!

MAKE ME FAITHFUL IN THE LITTLE THINGS, FATHER.

*So then, each of us will give an
account of himself to God.*

ROMANS 14:12 NIV

Has your supervisor ever given you an
assignment that was so important and so large
that you were the envy of the whole department?
You labored long and hard—giving it your best
effort. You felt honored with such responsibility.
You purposed to make your supervisor look good.
You wanted them to know you were worthy of
such trust.

On the other hand, have you ever been given
a small assignment that no one wanted to do?
Maybe you felt insulted and embarrassed by
having to do something so petty. You asked
yourself, *Is this all they think I am capable of
doing? Does this small job represent what they*

think of me?

Thank God for the small beginnings (Zechariah 4:10). Be trustworthy and faithful with the little and you will be the same way with much (Matthew 25:23). Then, not only will your supervisor say, "Well done!" but your Heavenly Father will too!

I can pray the breath prayer, *Make me faithful in the little things, Father,* when—

- I am given a large and important job.

- I am given a small and unimportant job.

- no one is watching me.

- I am in charge of money.

- I would rather be relaxing.

- others are depending on me.

- it is time to pay my bills.

Make me faithful in the little things, Father.

LORD, MAY I WALK IN YOUR PEACE.

My dear brothers, take note of this: Everyone should be quick to listen, slow to speak and slow to become angry, for man's anger does not bring about the righteous life that God desires.

JAMES 1:19-20 NIV

Many times it is the everyday, nothing-out-of-the-ordinary annoyances that cause you to want to "punch somebody's lights out."

Maybe it's the hectic bumper-to-bumper morning traffic, or the driver behind you who made an obscene gesture. Or perhaps you had to call the telephone company again this month to ask that they remove the same incorrect long-distance charge that was on last month's bill. And let's not forget the shopper with a loaded cart who rushes ahead of you to get in the checkout lane clearly marked "15 items or less."

Before you become angry or spout off something that you might regret, ask God to help you hold your peace. Retaliation does not please God but a strong witness brings Him glory.

I can pray the breath prayer, *Lord, may I walk in Your peace,* when—

- I am next in line and the cashier closes the checkout lane.

- a driver abruptly cuts in front of me.

- I am put on hold on the telephone.

- I have to repeatedly explain the same problem to different customer representatives before I get help.

- I am blamed for others' mistakes.

- others borrow my belongings without asking.

Lord, may I walk in Your peace.

THANK YOU FOR THE BEAUTY OF YOUR WORLD.

"You alone are the Lord. You made the heavens, even the highest heavens, and all their starry host, the earth and all that is on it, the seas and all that is in them."

NEHEMIAH 9:6 NIV

When was the last time you stopped long enough to smell the roses? Literally.

Aren't you thankful that God gave you senses so you can enjoy the beauty He created? It began when He saw that everything He created was good. In spite of man's mistakes, the beauty of creation is still evident: the fiery sun in the day and the luminous moon at night; the Big Dipper and the Little Dipper made up of stars and dazzling comet showers.

There are mountains, glaciers, deserts, and seas—each unique and teeming with life. But you are the masterpiece of God's creation—His unique design in every intricate detail. It is said that beauty is in the eye of the beholder, and God's eye is on you.

I can pray the breath prayer, *Thank You for the beauty of Your world,* when—

- I look at the different races of people.

- a baby is born.

- I walk through a garden.

- I walk along the beach.

- I look at a rainbow.

- I examine the sky at night.

- I stroll through a zoo.

Lord, thank You for the beauty of Your world.

MERCIFUL GOD, I WILL SEEK YOUR FACE.

O Lord . . . When You said,
"Seek My face," My heart said to You,
"Your face, Lord, I will seek."

PSALM 27:7-8 NKJV

Do you have a family member whom you can hardly wait to spend time with? The look on their face makes it so easy for you to share your heart with them.

Family might not be near you all the time. Not so with God. He loves His family, and He is there with them all the time. He desires to talk and fellowship with each of His children. The book of Genesis says that God visited Adam and Eve and talked with them, making their family complete.

God planned for Jesus to be the firstborn, with many brothers and sisters (Romans 8:28

NLT). You are God's child and His desire is for you to seek His face—enjoying talking and fellow-shipping with Him in the same way He desires to do with you.

Do not wait until you need to have a prayer answered. Talk with Him daily and look into His loving face.

I can pray the breath prayer, *Merciful God, I will seek Your face,* when—

- I wake up in the morning.

- I prepare for bed at night.

- I need confidence or assurance.

- I feel alone.

- I am thankful.

- I need to know Your will.

- as I go about my day.

Merciful God, I will seek Your face.

JESUS, KEEP ME IN YOUR PERFECT PEACE.

*Peace I leave with you; my peace
I give you. I do not give to you as
the world gives. Do not let your hearts
be troubled and do not be afraid.*

JOHN 14:27 NIV

Your Heavenly Father's desire is for you to be at peace with Him, within yourself, and with others. His peace is not the kind found in the world. The world's peace is unstable. Much of the time, you are surrounded with chaotic conditions and people who are stressed out.

Philippians 4:6-7 NLT says not to worry. Instead, you can pray. Tell God what you need and thank Him for what He has done. Then His peace, which is far more wonderful than the human mind can understand, will stand guard over your heart and your mind as you live in Christ Jesus.

Since Jesus has promised you this peace, you can rest in it right now. You can do that knowing everything is right with you and God. He promised to keep you in perfect peace when you trust Him and fix your thoughts on Him (Isaiah 26:3 NLT).

I can pray the breath prayer, *Jesus, keep me in Your perfect peace,* when—

- others annoy me.

- I am afraid.

- I hear bad news.

- others are worried.

- others refuse to be at peace with me.

- I am at home alone.

  Jesus, keep me in Your perfect peace.

OPEN MY MIND TO UNDERSTAND YOUR WORD, GOD.

Then He opened their minds to understand the Scriptures.

MARK 24:45 NASB

"I just don't understand you!" "Do you understand what I'm saying?" "I'm sorry that I misunderstood." So many things that occur are the result of bad communication.

You cannot walk in God's ways if you do not understand them. But God has sent His Holy Spirit to teach you about the Bible and to lead you to the truth. 2 Timothy 2:15 AMP says to study God's Word, correctly analyze it, accurately divide it, rightly handle it, and then skillfully teach it. God calls you to do this because He has also equipped you to be able to do it. Ask for insight and He will give it.

Your Heavenly Father knows that you cannot obey His will and live the prosperous life He planned for you if you do not fully understand His Word. Ask Him to open up your mind and give you insight and understanding. The things He shows you will change your life in wonderful ways.

I can pray the breath prayer, *Open my mind to understand Your Word, God,* when—

- I study the Bible.

- Your Word is preached.

- You want to tell me something.

- someone asks me about Your Word.

- I need guidance.

- life is confusing.

Open my mind to understand Your Word, God.

I WILL SLEEP IN YOUR SAFETY, LORD OF ALL.

I will lie down and sleep in peace,
for you alone, O Lord,
make me dwell in safety.

PSALM 4:8 NIV

"Tossin' and turnin', turnin' and tossin',
tossin' and turnin' all night."

Do these words, taken from a popular song
from the 1950s, describe the way your nights
have been lately? If so, you are not sleeping in
peace. A good night's sleep is necessary for a
clear head and a healthy body.

God does not want you staying up late or
getting up early because you are stressed out over
problems. He does not desire that you lose sleep

because you are in pain or worried. It pleases Him when you are prosperous and in good health.

Psalm 121:3 says God watches over you and He will not sleep. So trust His watchful care and go to sleep.

I can pray the breath prayer, *I will sleep in Your safety, Lord of all,* when—

- I am home alone.

- I am in an unfamiliar place.

- I have a lot to do tomorrow.

- there is a storm.

- I hear frightful news.

- I am sick.

- I am restless.

- I am excited.

I will sleep in Your safety, Lord of all.

SHINE YOUR FACE ON ME, FATHER.

The Lord make His face to shine upon and enlighten you; . . . the Lord lift up His [approving] countenance upon you.

NUMBERS 6:25-26 AMP

Have you ever said good morning to a neighbor or coworker only to have them mumble an almost inaudible reply while scowling? Your first thought may be to look away from such unpleasantness.

Then again, maybe you have spoken to someone whose face lit up as they responded cheerfully? No doubt you dreaded seeing the first person again but looked forward to seeing the second one.

You can look forward to seeing God.

Israelite high priests blessed all the people who asked God to smile and look with pleasure upon them. And if God asks us to ask for something, He means to make it come true.

Your Heavenly Father loves you. Imagine how pleased He is with you as He nods approvingly in your direction.

I can pray the breath prayer, *Shine Your face on me, Father,* when—

- others turn their faces from me.

- gloom seems to envelop me.

- others disapprove of me.

- I know I've done my best.

- I feel discouraged.

- I cannot seem to find my way.

   Shine Your face on me, Father.

I NEED YOUR GENTLENESS, GOD.

Like a shepherd . . . He will gently lead.

ISAIAH 40:11 NLT

God's love is what drew you to Him. He is a good and kind Father who blesses His children.

He sent us a loving Savior who humbly bore the sins of the world. His compassion caused Him to heal the brokenhearted and offer deliverance and rest from oppression and burdens.

His gentle nature drew little children to Him. He willingly fed the hungry—whether they hungered for natural food or for the heart of God. The Bible says He understands and sympathizes with your weaknesses because He was tempted in every way as you are.

Right now, regardless of any problem you

might have, your Heavenly Father's tender mercies are over you. He is tenderly covering you just like a hen covers her chicks (Psalm 91).

So, do what Elijah did after he went through a mighty windstorm, an earthquake, and fire. Listen for God's gentle whisper (1 Kings 19:12 NLT). He desires to see His gentleness active in your life. Trust His gentleness to make you great (Psalm 18:35).

I can pray the breath prayer, *I need Your gentleness, God,* when—

- I become angry.

- others treat me harshly.

- I have a rough day at work.

- my heart feels heavy.

- I feel pushed aside.

- I am sick.

I need Your gentleness, God.

MY HEART YEARS FOR YOU, GOD.

As the deer pants for streams of water,
so I long for You, O God.

PSALM 42:1 NLT

Have you ever been so desperate for chocolate that you can almost taste it? Maybe you want a particular piece of clothing so badly you sometimes picture yourself wearing it.

A substitute can never take the place of the real thing. When you can't take it anymore, at times you might do whatever is necessary to get it.

David's desire for God was like that. The Psalms describe his fervent love for God. He was a king, yet he humbly acknowledged how much he needed God and longed for His presence.

God loves you and chose you to be His child.

You live, move, and exist in Him (Acts 17:28 NLT). Deep inside, there is a part of your life that only He can satisfy. He promised that when you seek Him with all your heart, you find Him.

I can pray the breath prayer, *My heart yearns for You, God,* when—

- I pray.

- I read Your Word.

- I am lonely.

- I am in distress.

- I need guidance.

- nothing else can satisfy my longing heart.

- I'm tempted to desire something else more than You.

   My heart yearns for You, God.

LORD, CAUSE MY FAITH TO GROW.

Faith comes from hearing the message, and the message is heard through the word of Christ.

ROMANS 10:17 NIV

Do you believe something because you repeatedly hear it or because of your confidence in the person who said it? Just because you hear something over and over again does not mean it is true. Gossip is a good example of that. But when someone you know personally, who has a sterling reputation for being honest—in word and deed—says something, you do not hesitate to believe it.

Christ Jesus exemplified the Word of God because He was the Word of God (John 1:14

NLT). He spoke only the truth. God's Word is truth (John 17:17) and the Bible is God's written Word. As a Christian, you can trust God's Word because you can trust Him. And the more you hear of His truth, the more your faith in His goodness and faithfulness grows.

I can pray the breath prayer, *Lord, cause my faith to grow,* when—

- I read Your Word.

- I obey Your Word.

- I need understanding and wisdom.

- I pray for others.

- I'm going through hard times.

Lord, cause my faith to grow.

LORD, DEFEND MY INTEGRITY.

I have been found innocent in his sight.
And I have not wronged you.

DANIEL 6:22 NLT

How do you handle it when others lie about you? After the initial shock wears off, you are probably angry and hurt.

Why would they do that to me? you might wonder. Particularly when you know what was said about you was not true.

In your heart, you know that God does not want you to be bitter and vengeful. But your mind tells you that you should defend yourself.

Do not worry. God will vindicate you because of your integrity (Psalm 26:1 NASB). He hates lying, and He will prove your accusers wrong (Isaiah 54:17 AMP). If He wants you to say something, believe that He will tell you what to say and when to say it (Luke 12:11-12 NIV). He will restore your good reputation.

I can pray the breath prayer, *Lord, defend my integrity,* when—

- I am falsely accused.

- others believe I am guilty.

- others lie about me.

- all evidence points to me.

- I cannot defend myself.

Lord, defend my integrity.

GUIDE ME IN THIS DECISION, FATHER.

Trust in the LORD with all your heart and lean not on your own understanding.

PROVERB 3:5 NIV

Decisions, decisions, decisions.

Not a day goes by that you are not faced with decisions of one kind or another. Some are easy ones. But then there are difficult ones that can leave you at a standstill, confused, or even feeling helpless.

Should I put Mother into a nursing home? Can I really afford to buy a new car right now? Do I take this new job, even though it means moving halfway across the country?

Life changes are not easy ones to make, but your Heavenly Father, the God of all wisdom, stands ready to give you that same wisdom. Then, when you are faced with decisions, you can know He will guide your steps.

You have the mind of Jesus Christ. His thoughts are your thoughts. When you call on Him, He will help you make right decisions.

I can pray the breath prayer, *Guide me in this decision, Father,* when—

- my family's future is at stake.

- I face controversy.

- someone asks a favor.

- I am dealing with my children.

- my spouse and I do not agree.

- others need my advice.

Guide me in this decision, Father.

SHOW ME YOUR GRACE, LORD

*Let us then approach the throne of grace
with confidence, so that we may receive mercy
and find grace to help us in our time of need.*

HEBREWS 4:16 NIV

"I did it again."

Sounds familiar, doesn't it?

You make a mistake, cry out to God with a promise never to do it again, and what happens? You find yourself right back on your knees in confession because you made the same dumb mistake again.

Will He forgive you? Of course He will.

God said He made you so it is no surprise to Him that you mess up every now and then. That's why He made provision for you to confess your faults, receive forgiveness, and get things right with Him. That is His grace. And it is His grace that will make you able to walk in His ways in the future.

It does not please God when we do wrong. But it makes Him happy when we choose to skip the pity party and instead go to Him for mercy, forgiveness, grace—and His strength to help us overcome mistakes in the future.

When you mess up, just 'fess up. God already knows about it anyway and is ready to offer His grace.

I can pray the breath prayer, *Show me Your grace, Lord,* when—

- I forget to walk in love.

- I hurt someone's feelings.

- I fail to do what is right.

- I get angry and say foolish things.

- I am weak.

- I am in trouble.

Show me Your grace, Lord.

MAKE ME STEADFAST IN YOUR WORD, GOD.

*You will keep in perfect
peace him whose mind is steadfast,
because he trusts in you.*

ISAIAH 26:3 NIV

There are times when it seems as if nothing can go wrong. The family is healthy. The job is going great. Then, suddenly the bottom drops out. The car breaks down, your boss chews you out, or you have a fight with your best friend.

Life is not without controversy and turmoil, but it is possible to live a life filled with peace by knowing God's Word and keeping your mind on Him.

The Bible is filled with instructions designed to help you live a successful, peaceful life. Reading your Bible plants God's Word in your head and in your heart. It is not only a tool to use for spiritual growth, but it is a weapon to fight adversity.

God has your back.

I can pray the breath prayer, *Make me steadfast in Your Word, God,* when—

- I am afraid.

- friends turn against me.

- I don't know which way to turn.

- there are too many questions without answers.

- nothing seems to be going right.

- sickness has attacked my body.

Make me steadfast in Your Word, God.

LORD, HELP ME HEAR YOUR VOICE.

I heard the voice of the Lord.

ISAIAH 6:8 NASB

Do you remember the chats you had with your parents or grandparents when you were a young child? Do you recall how they patiently and lovingly told you what to say or do in certain circumstances? Soon, you began to consult teachers and guidance counselors at school. Perhaps you had other adults that you confided in, as well as siblings and your best friends.

As you grew up, you became less dependent on the advice of others. However, one voice you should always be open to is God's. He will help you learn to know His voice (John 10:4). His advice, instruction, and even correction can stop frustration and confusion. Take time to ask God to help you hear Him and then take some time to sit still in the quiet and really listen.

I can pray the breath prayer, *Lord, help me hear Your voice,* when—

- I need clear direction.

- I begin to feel confused.

- many others are telling me what to do.

- I have to make a quick decision.

- others ask me for advice.

- I need a quiet moment with you.

Lord, help me hear Your voice.

LORD, HELP ME OVERCOME EVIL WITH GOOD.

Don't let evil get the best of you;
get the best of evil by doing good.

ROMANS 12:21 MSG

Abuse, bigotry, prejudice, injustice, oppression—all these stem from hatred. But they do not necessarily have to relate to your natural heritage. The one thing they have in common is their assault on your dignity, your self-respect, and your self-worth.

More than likely, your first inclination would be to strike back at someone who hurt or humiliated you. The world considers it a sign of weakness or cowardice when you do not defend yourself or try to get even.

However, this is what God calls us to do. And only God can give you the love and strength to do that. He's already put that ability in you because God, the greater One who lives in you, is greater than the one in the world that opposes you. Let the goodness of God overflow from your life into the lives of others.

1 Peter 3:9 NLT says, "Don't repay evil for evil. Don't retaliate when people say unkind things about you. Instead, pay them back with a blessing. That is what God wants you to do, and He will bless you for it."

I can pray the breath prayer, *Lord, help me overcome evil with good*, when—

- others insult me.

- I desire to get even.

- others encourage me to strike back.

- others say I am a coward because I do not strike back.

- people belittle me.

- I feel inadequate.

Lord, help me overcome evil with good.

MAKE ME A BLESSING TO OTHERS, FATHER.

I will bless you . . . and I will make you a blessing to others.

GENESIS 12:2 NLT

In the hustle and bustle of daily life, do you sometimes focus on your own needs so much that you forget that others have needs too? It is easy to do when you read that the economy is unstable, large corporations are folding, and lay-offs are increasing. You feel that taking care of your own family is hard enough.

The book of Genesis has a good example of how one person can be used to help others. It recounts how Joseph, Jacob's well-beloved son, was imprisoned unjustly in Egypt. But God gave him favor with Pharaoh and prospered whatever

Joseph put his hands to so that his family and Israel were fed and taken care of during a terrible famine.

God has promised to take care of you and to bless you. But He does not want you to forget others. Be sensitive to God's voice. Even if what you have seems small, be willing to follow His direction and help others who are in need.

I can pray the breath prayer, *Make me a blessing to others, Father,* when—

- I do not seem to have enough for my needs.

- I have more than enough for my needs.

- no one else will help.

- their need is more than just money.

- they do not ask for help.

Make me a blessing to others, Father.

LORD, DISPLAY YOUR SELF-CONTROL THROUGH ME.

The fruit of the Spirit is love, joy, peace, patience, kindness, goodness, faithfulness, gentleness and self-control.

GALATIANS 5:22-23 NIV

Have you ever let your emotions get the best of you in a heated situation? Perhaps your head said, "Tell it like it is," but your heart said, "Show compassion." Perhaps you wanted to stop but your emotions were in control and you didn't stop.

God wants us to practice self-control. When you lead with your heart, compassion for others comes before your own motives. Self-control brings peace into heated situations. Sometimes it's difficult to harness your emotions and wait

for others to see the gifts and talents you have;
but when you practice self-control, God brings
your gifts and talents to the forefront in a way
that others appreciate and admire.

When you are struggling to give your heart
first place in your life, ask God to help you
exercise self-control.

I can pray the breath prayer, *Lord, display Your
self-control through me,* when—

- I eat and drink.

- I shop.

- I work.

- I compete in sports or games.

- I get excited.

- I feel impatient.

- someone is rude to me.

- someone tries to argue with me.

Lord, display Your self-control through me.

BE MY FATHER.

*"I will be a Father to you,
and you will be my sons and daughters,
says the Lord Almighty."*

2 CORINTHIANS 6:18 NIV

How do you describe a true father? Is he a protector? Provider? Teacher? Helper? Confidant? Defender? Disciplinarian? Do you picture him as someone who would sacrifice himself for you without giving it a second thought? Would he let you know that nothing is too good for you?

Is he dependable? Truthful? Forgiving? Patient? Compassionate? Good-natured?

All of these attributes describe God's character.

Regardless of who you are or what you have done, God calls you His child when you believe and confess Jesus as your Lord. Romans 8:38-39 says that nothing will be able to separate you from His love.

Love, honor, and pray for your natural father, realizing that he is not perfect in every way. Love, honor, and praise your Heavenly Father, acknowledging that He is perfect in every way. He sees you as His child and wants you to see Him as your loving Heavenly Father.

I can pray the breath prayer, *Be my Father,* when—

- my natural father is not with me.

- I need a strong arm to lean on.

- I need fatherly advice.

- I need to hear that everything is going to be all right.

- I need to be comforted.

- I need to feel safe and secure.

Be my Father.

LORD, LET ME TRADE IN COMPLAINING FOR PRAISE.

Bless the LORD, O my soul;
And all that is within me
bless His holy name.
PSALM 103:1 NASB

No matter how optimistic you are, you should realize that life is not going to be a bed of roses every day. Eventually, you deal with unpleasantness—a person, place, or thing. What is important is how you handle it.

Do you feel sorry for yourself? Blame others? Become angry?

God promised the Israelites a bountiful and rich land when He brought them out of slavery to the Egyptians. His desire was that they would rest and enjoy the abundance of His love and provision. However, they soon forgot their miraculous delivery and began to complain. (Read the book of Numbers.) They complained against Moses, their God-given leader, and worst of all, they complained against God!

The Bible says they suffered terrible things, including death, during their forty-year journey because they did not trust and obey God.

Your Heavenly Father will take care of you and help you manage your problems if you trust and obey Him. When you trade your complaints for praise, it opens the door for God to deliver you into His goodness.

I can pray the breath prayer, *Lord, let me trade in complaining for praise,* when—

- I am disappointed.
- situations become uncomfortable.
- I am sick.
- I am in need.
- I am tired.
- I am mistreated.
- You do not seem to answer my prayers soon enough.

Lord, let me trade in complaining for praise.

MAKE ME WHOLE, JESUS.

"I will restore you to health and heal your wounds," declares the Lord.

JEREMIAH 30:17 NIV

Pollution. Acid rain. Oil spills. Mercury poisoning. Pesticides. Growth hormones. Secondhand smoke. Radiation. Radon. Carbon monoxide. Chemical warfare. Global warming. Is anything safe anymore? Can we really trust the foods that we eat? Does anyone really know what is good for us, and is it even possible to enjoy good health to a ripe old age?

The answer is yes. Almighty God knows all things, and He has given you His Word. Ask for His wisdom so that you can make the right decisions regarding your health. He has promised

116

His blessings on your food and water (Exodus 23:25 NIV). He promised that no weapon formed against you would prosper (Isaiah 54:17 NASB).

God is your refuge and fortress and He has ordered His angels to protect you (Psalm 91:2,11). He does not want you to be afraid. Believe His Word so that you will be satisfied with a long life (Psalm 91:16).

I can pray the breath prayer, *Make me whole, Jesus*, when—

- sickness "is going around."

- I have a physical examination.

- I start my family.

- I travel during vacation.

- I begin getting older.

- I go out to eat.

Make me whole, Jesus.

FORGIVE ME, FATHER.

*If we confess our sins, he is faithful
and just and will forgive us our sins and
purify us from all unrighteousness.*

1 JOHN 1:9 NIV

How many times have you heard someone
say, "Nobody's perfect"?

Believe it or not, it's true. As long as you are
in the world, you are capable of making mistakes.

Your Heavenly Father knew you would
make mistakes. That is why He so graciously
provided the way for you to be forgiven and stay
in fellowship with Him.

Because you are a Christian, God requires
you to ask forgiveness when you do something
wrong—knowingly or unknowingly, intentionally
or unintentionally. Justifying your actions, making
excuses, and blaming someone or something
else—these do not absolve you. God holds you

accountable for your actions toward Him, others, and yourself.

"I'm not hurting anyone but myself!" you say. But do you realize how dear you are to God's heart? Christ Jesus died for you! God wants you to treat yourself with love too.

His Word gives explicit instructions regarding your conduct. When you disobey in any way, be quick to ask His forgiveness. And He will be just as quick to forgive you.

I can pray the breath prayer, *Forgive me, Father,* when—

- I disobey You.

- I mistreat others.

- I mistreat myself.

- I disobey the law.

- I blame others for my wrongdoing.

- I cause someone to do something wrong.

Forgive me, Father.

FATHER, GIVE ME YOUR GENEROUS HEART.

All the believers were one in heart and mind. No one claimed that any of his possessions was his own, but they shared everything they had.

ACTS 4:32 NIV

"That's mine! Give it to me!" toddlers often say.

"But what about me?" adults ask more often than they should. It seems as if we are born with a spirit of self-preservation, always looking out for number one.

When you were a baby, the slightest whimper and whine caused concerned faces to peer into your crib. It really was all about you. But as you grew older, you discovered how to take care of yourself.

The thought, *If I don't look out for myself, no one else will,* is not in line with God's way of doing things. Be sure you are not so tightly wrapped up in yourself that your heart is not open to others' pains and needs. When you gladly share your talents and skills, your time and possessions to help others, God is pleased and will certainly see to it that you are taken care of.

I can pray the breath prayer, *Father, give me Your generous heart,* when—

- it is time to give an offering in church.

- I am asked for a donation.

- I am asked to volunteer at a shelter for the homeless.

- a coworker does not have money for lunch.

- a coworker needs a ride to work.

- my neighborhood has a charity drive.

- a friend needs a place to stay because of a power blackout.

Father, give me Your generous heart.

LORD, MAKE ME A CHEERFUL GIVER.

*You must each make up your own mind
as to how much you should give. Don't give
reluctantly or in response to pressure.
For God loves the person who gives cheerfully.*

2 CORINTHIANS 9:7 NLT

What is your attitude when God tells you to share? Would it be easier for you if you had more to give? The amount you give does not touch God's heart as much as your willingness to obey Him.

The Bible says that whatever measure you use in giving—large or small—will be used to measure what is given back to you (Luke 6:38 NLT).

Be like the young boy with the five loaves and two fish who willingly gave it all to Christ

Jesus to feed more than five thousand people. After everyone had eaten, there was some left (John 6:9-13). Willingly give as God leads you, whether it is a little or a lot. God will return it to you in full measure and running over (Luke 6:38).

I can pray the breath prayer, *Lord, make me a cheerful giver,* when—

- I see someone in need.

- someone asks for my time.

- someone needs my energy.

- I have a little.

- I have a lot.

- You haven't even asked me to give.

Lord, make me a cheerful giver.

I HONOR YOU, GOD.

Now to the King of eternity, incorruptible and immortal, invisible, the only God, be honor and glory forever and ever.

1 TIMOTHY 1:17 AMP

As you grew up you saw actors, singers, and sports stars whom you dreamed of being like. You probably mimicked the way they looked or talked or dressed.

Now that you are grown, you still have favorite actors, singers, and sports stars. But you have matured to the point where those whom you respect and highly esteem now might include those in the fields of religion, politics, science, law, or medicine. These are the ones who affect your real life and inspire you to handle it with gravity.

The Bible says to give respect and honor to whomever it is due (Romans 13:7 NLT). God deserves the highest honor. He created the men and women of whom you think so highly. He is the Giver of life—natural and eternal. He is loving, wise, merciful, and compassionate. He is also faithful, truthful, invincible, and wealthy. He says you are His child, so give your Heavenly Father the honor He is due.

I can pray the breath prayer, *I honor You, God,* when—

- I worship You.
- I praise You.
- I obey You.
- I'm angry at Your decision and want to remember that You are my King.
- I pull aside from my busy schedule to spend time with You.
- I tell others about You.
- I desire to please You.

I honor You, God.

I praise You, God Most High.

All Your works shall praise You,
O Lord, and Your loving ones shall bless
You [affectionately and gratefully shall
your saints confess and praise You]!

Psalm 145:10 AMP

During the day, people are busy taking care of their affairs—talking on cell phones, driving, shopping, eating, filling their gas tanks without so much as taking time to look up. A thunderous jet, held up by God's supernatural power, streaks across the sky like a giant silver bird. You take a deep, satisfied breath and say, "Dear Lord, I praise You for Your wonderful works because they are truly marvelous!"(See Psalm 118:23.)

The Bible says that everything that has breath is to praise God (Psalm 150:6). More than that, it says that all of nature—including mountains, pastures, valleys, seas, and the forests—are to praise Him!

His heart desires for His people to praise Him because praise opens our eyes to see Him and grow our faith. Much applause and praise is given to man for his accomplishments. How much more should our praise be lifted up to the God who has all power and all virtue?

Be thankful that you know He is great and that He has given you a heart filled with great praises for Him.

I can pray the breath prayer, *I praise You, God Most High,* when—

- I admire the great works of Your hands.
- I start a new day.
- I am tired and frustrated.
- I close my eyes to rest.
- everything is going well.
- I realize my life is Your creation.

I praise You, God Most High.

LORD, ALL I AM
IS FROM YOU.

Whoever lives in Me and I in him
bears much (abundant) fruit. However,
apart from Me [cut off from vital
union with Me] you can do nothing.

JOHN 15:5 AMP

You're feeling pretty good about yourself.

You just signed the papers on your first home. The car you've always dreamed of owning will be yours in just a few short days. And in all probability that promotion will come sooner than you thought because your supervisor is leaving. When you stop and think about it, you have done pretty well for yourself in a very short time.

Stop! Hold on just one minute.

Exactly *who* is it that has done well?

The reality is that God ordered your steps and showed you the path to take to reach this successful destination. He was there to comfort you, to encourage you, and to provide for you. Don't push Him aside; give Him the credit. Your success is a declaration of His faithfulness to you.

I can pray the breath prayer, *Lord, all I am is from You*, when—

- I take credit for my accomplishments.

- I think I am so gifted and talented.

- I fail to give you the glory.

- I don't recognize You in my life.

- my ego starts to get the best of me.

- I think I am better than others.

Lord, all I am is from You.

YOU ARE GOD OVER ALL AND MY FATHER.

Cease striving and know that I am God.

PSALM 46:10 NASB

What's on the agenda today? Meetings. Quick decisions. Lunch with a client. Project deadlines.

It's a never-ending cycle. And none of it serves to make you a healthier person—physically or spiritually.

Maybe you need to slow down for a moment. Relax, take a deep breath, and ask yourself, *Who's in charge here, anyway?*

Psalm 37:23 AMP says, "The steps of a [good] man are directed and established by the Lord when He delights in his way [and He busies Himself with his every step]." God is watching over you. He knows what's on the agenda today, and He has already taken time to plan it out so that it will be easy for you.

If you are stressed out, take a time-out with God and trust Him to lead the way.

I can pray the breath prayer, *You are God over all and my Father,* when—

- I have so much to do.

- I feel overwhelmed.

- I can't think straight.

- I don't know which direction to go.

- there's more to do than I can handle.

- there is no order in my life.

  You are God over all and my Father.

SPEAK YOUR WORDS THROUGH ME, LORD.

Do not worry about what to say or how to say it.

MATTHEW 10:19 NIV

How many times has someone come to you for advice and you didn't know quite what to say? The fact that they came to you is a sign that they trust you. They have confidence in the words you speak. That's why it is important to always give answers that line up with God's Word. Say the wrong thing, and it could cause someone to stumble or fall.

Jesus told the disciples that He did not speak on His own initiative, but that God had told Him what to say and how to say it (John 12:49 NASB). The words He spoke brought life to every situation.

When you are in tune with God and His

Word, then you won't have a problem giving advice or offering words of encouragement when someone comes knocking. Then you can be sure that when you open your mouth the words are His.

I can pray the breath prayer, *Speak Your words through me, Lord,* when—

- I really don't know what to say.

- I want to encourage someone.

- I am trying to bring peace to a stressful situation.

- someone needs to hear Your Word.

- I need to defend myself, or my actions.

- I need to discipline my child.

- I want to make peace with my spouse.

Speak Your words through me, Lord.

HELP ME TO SEE YOUR CAUTION FLAG.

*Test the spirits to see whether they
are from God, because many false prophets
have gone out into the world.*

1 JOHN 4:1 NIV

Have you ever started work on a new job
and found kind and helpful coworkers? "The
supply cabinet is right over there, and here's the
copier," one might point out.

But what about the ones whose mission, it
seems, is to warn you about all the pitfalls of the
job? "Watch out for so-and-so." "You can't trust
that one over there." "You'd better watch your
back."

While their motives may be pure, the Bible
says they stir up strife. If you're not watchful,

you can quickly find yourself right where they are —complaining, criticizing, and spreading unfounded rumors.

In Proverbs 6:19, strife is identified as one of the things God hates. You should do whatever is necessary to avoid it. Observe people for yourself. God will help you recognize when someone is sincere or if they are trying to stir up trouble.

Be led by the Spirit of God.

I can pray the breath prayer, *Help me to see Your caution flag,* when—

- someone warns me to "watch out!"

- I am quick to listen to what others say.

- others try to control my thinking.

- nothing seems to be going right.

- sickness has attacked my body

- I feel like no one cares

Help me to see Your caution flag.

Make me watchful, Father.

"Be always on the watch, and pray that you may be able to escape all that is about to happen, and that you may be able to stand before the Son of Man."

Luke 21:36 NIV

You're sitting at a traffic light when all of a sudden the driver in the car behind you starts blowing his horn. You look, and the light is green. Your supervisor asks you a question but gets no response because you're daydreaming.

A doctor might suggest you're a victim of Attention Deficit Disorder (ADD) or some other problem that causes people not to pay attention. But it could simply be a matter of redirecting your thoughts.

Maybe you just need to slow down and focus. Or, maybe you need to take better care of your body. Getting the proper amount of rest will help you stay alert. That means going to bed on time, getting some exercise, and eating the proper foods.

The Bible says your body is God's dwelling place (1 Corinthians 3:16) and that His mind is in you (1 Corinthians 2:16).

Just as His thoughts are always clear, yours can also be clear.

I can pray the breath prayer, *Make me watchful, Father,* when—

- I am driving in traffic.

- others are talking.

- the minister is preaching.

- someone is giving me important instructions.

- I'm really not interested.

- I think nothing is going on.

Make me watchful, Father.

GIVE ME ENDURANCE, LORD.

I press on toward the goal to win the [supreme and heavenly] prize to which God in Christ Jesus is calling us upward.

PHILIPPIANS 3:14 AMP

How many times have you been ready to give up, throw in the towel, and quit? Life, with its many challenges, is filled with opportunities for us to walk away from things because they seem too difficult. Even the simplest things such as the challenges presented by some of today's video games are enough to make you want to turn tail and run.

Don't give up! In Philippians, the apostle Paul spoke of the many challenges he faced while preaching the Gospel. He recognized his own imperfections and his weaknesses and readily acknowledged them. But he would not allow them to stop him from reaching his goal—the prize that only Jesus Christ could award.

Sure, times get tough. But Jesus said when we feel weak and tired, we can rest in Him (Matthew 11:28). We can draw from His power, which He said is made perfect in our weakness (2 Corinthians 12:9).

Press forward. Reach deep into your spirit. Go to the One who is able to sustain you and give you the strength to attain your goal.

I can pray the breath prayer, *Give me endurance, Lord,* when—

- I am tired.

- I have done all I can do.

- others around me are still trying.

- I am about to lose confidence in myself.

- I get behind and don't think I can catch up.

- I really don't want to keep trying.

Give me endurance, Lord.

MAY I ACCEPT YOUR LOVING DISCIPLINE, FATHER

*"Don't ignore it when the Lord disciplines you,
and don't be discouraged when he corrects you.
For the Lord disciplines those He loves."*

HEBREWS 12:5-6 NLT

Neither discipline nor correction is comfortable. They both represent that you have done something wrong, which is rather hard for most people to admit. The disciples of Christ Jesus were willing to follow Him and learn from Him. This meant they had to humbly accept His instructions and discipline if they really wanted to do the things He did.

They had different personalities and temperaments, came from different backgrounds, and did different work. Christ Jesus wisely saw past their "rough edges" and patiently taught and disciplined them—sometimes rather sternly.

Sometimes He had to demonstrate "tough love" to encourage their faith, but they trusted Him because they knew that He loved them.

You are God's child—a disciple—and you desire to obey Him because you love Him. As you study His Word and pray, He will teach you, instruct you, and discipline you. Humbly accept those things, even if you feel a little uncomfortable, knowing that He loves you and desires only the best for you.

I can pray the breath prayer, *May I accept Your loving discipline, Father,* when—

- I say the wrong thing.

- I do the wrong thing.

- I make a wrong choice.

- I mistreat others.

- my attitude is wrong.

- I do not want to admit that I am wrong.

May I accept Your loving discipline, Father.

HELP ME TO REMEMBER THAT I AM FREE, JESUS.

*It was for freedom that Christ set us free;
therefore keep standing firm and do not
be subject again to a yoke of slavery.*

GALATIANS 5:1 NASB

Not many people can read historical accounts of slavery and not feel some kind of sadness or remorse. How horrible life must have been for those who were held in captivity, never free to come and go as they pleased or to make their own decisions.

Believe it or not, before you became a Christian you were just like a slave. The Bible says you were a "captive" (Luke 4:18) who walked around in darkness, blinded to the truth.

But in His loving-kindness, Christ Jesus came to free you from the bondage of captivity and sin and to transform your life into a brand new one filled with joy and hope. When you gave your life to Christ, the shackles of sin dropped off. The chains of guilt were broken. And the love of God came in and took up residence.

No longer are you a slave, but you are free—free to love, free to worship, and free to praise your Heavenly Father. Jesus released you from sin's captivity. You are free!

I can pray the breath prayer, *Help me to remember that I am free, Jesus,* when—

- I am reminded of my past.

- others want to run my life.

- I feel trapped in my job.

- I am faced with difficult decisions.

- I start to feel condemnation.

- I need answers.

Help me to remember that I am free, Jesus.

FATHER, HELP ME TO HOLD ON TO YOU.

Take hold of the eternal life to which you were called when you made your good confession in the presence of many witnesses.

1 TIMOTHY 6:12 NIV

Ever noticed how close a small child will stick to his mother while walking the aisles inside a grocery store? If the mother stops, the child quickly grabs hold of her. It's his assurance that she will not get away from him.

By the same token, the mother is usually clinging to that child, holding his hand tightly to make sure he doesn't stray.

That's how God is toward us. When you became a Christian, He came to live inside you through His Spirit. You can't get any closer than that! You never have to feel alone or unloved. Not when God assures you through His Word that He will never leave you or forsake you.

Reach out in your spirit right now and touch Him. Touch Him through a song. Touch Him through a prayer. Touch Him through His Word. And when you touch Him, hold on awhile and let His love fill you to overflowing.

It pleases Him when you do that.

I can pray the breath prayer, *Father, help me to hold on to You,* when—

- I feel I'm about to fall.

- others criticize me.

- my best is not good enough.

- I'm feeling lonely.

- I can't seem to get ahead.

Father, help me to hold on to You.

LORD, I ACKNOWLEDGE YOUR BLESSINGS.

All these blessings will come upon you and accompany you if you obey the Lord your God.

DEUTERONOMY 28:2 NIV

If everything has been going well for you, it is not just a coincidence. As a child of God, you reap the benefits of His blessings. It is because you are living in obedience to His Word, that God is willing to do such wonderful things for you.

Do you realize how blessed you are that God the Father loves you so much? Are you thankful? Then why not tell Him? Take time out to count your blessings and see what the Lord has done for you. Then, thank Him for loving you so much.

Don't forget to remember where all your blessings come from.

I can pray the breath prayer, *Lord, I acknowledge Your blessings*, when—

- I try to take credit for my accomplishments.

- I start to feel proud.

- I am feeling helpless.

- I start to have a pity party.

- I am envious of others.

- I start to complain.

    Lord, I acknowledge Your blessings.

FATHER, LEAD ME AWAY FROM TEMPTATION AND DELIVER ME FROM EVIL.

"Keep alert and pray. Otherwise temptation will overpower you. For though the spirit is willing enough, the body is weak!"

MATTHEW 26:41 NLT

You know you do not need that second doughnut. You know you should not revisit the bar where you and your friends used to hang out. Your conscience tells you to return the twenty-dollar bill the cashier gave you by mistake. Why does temptation face you wherever you turn?

Do not panic! You're not alone. When you accepted Christ you changed, and so did your lifestyle—but the world is still the same. Temptation is still lurking.

1 Corinthians 10:13 NLT says the temptations you encounter are no different from those that others face. God is faithful to keep them from

becoming so strong that you cannot stand up against them. He will show you a way out so that you will not give in to them.

Christ Jesus also faced temptation, so He understands your burden. Go to the throne of your Heavenly Father and receive His mercy and grace to help you find a way out of temptation (Hebrews 4:15-16). He has already prepared a way of escape.

I can pray the breath prayer, *Father, lead me away from temptation and deliver me from evil,* when—

- I know someone is watching.
- I am with others.
- I eat or drink.
- I enjoy entertainment.
- I meet an attractive person.
- I am driving.
- I do my taxes.

Father, lead me away from temptation and deliver me from evil.

LEAD ME, LORD.

Since You are my rock and my fortress,
for the sake of your name lead and guide me.

PSALM 31:3 NIV

Notice the trust a blind person has in his guide dog or the person who leads him while walking. Whenever the guide moves, stops, or turns, the blind person does the same without question or delay. He relies on the sight and skill of his companion to help him reach his destination safely. In a way, his life is in their care.

2 Corinthians 5:7 NIV says that Christians live by faith, not by sight—like the blind. Just as they depend on the help of a guide, you need the Lord to lead and guide you.

He knows the answers and solutions to your questions, perplexities, and problems. He knows if you should make a move or just stand still. He orders your steps according to His Word (Psalm 119:133) and prevents your feet from slipping (Psalm 37:31 NIV). His Word is a lamp for your feet and a light for your path (Psalm 119:105). Trust Him and allow Him to be your guide.

I can pray the breath prayer, *Lead me, Lord,* when—

- I am confused.

- I have questions.

- I am hesitant.

- I am offered a new job.

- others follow me.

- I am driving and I get lost.

- I have a difficult decision to make.

Lead me, Lord.

MAY I REST IN YOU, SAVIOR.

We are pressed on every side . . .
but we are not crushed and broken.

2 CORINTHIANS 4:8 NLT

You have bills to pay and people to pay attention to. Your yard needs tending and so does your house. The clothes need to be washed and so does your car. Your son needs a haircut and so does your dog. The list goes on and on and on, as does life.

"There's only one of me!" you cry. You are near tears when you suddenly think how relieved you are that God—not you—runs the universe. Boy, talk about pressure! *How do You do it, Father?* you wonder. You realize that if anyone has the answer to your dilemma, He does.

His Word invites you to go to Him when you are weary and burdened and He will give you rest. He will give you wisdom to know what to let go of (James 1:5) and the strength to handle the rest (Philippians 4:13). He does not desire that you try to carry the weight of the world on your shoulders. He is already upholding it and maintaining it by His mighty Word of power (Hebrews 1:3 AMP).

I can pray the breath prayer, *May I rest in You, Savior,* when—

- I have a close deadline to meet.
- I am stalled in heavy traffic and late for a meeting.
- I am very tired.
- I have a lot to do and not enough time to do it.
- I have an important assignment.
- I have to speak before a large group of people.
- I am sick and cannot afford to miss work.

May I rest in You, Savior.

HEAR MY CRY, LORD.

This poor man cried, and the Lord heard him and saved him out of all his troubles.

PSALM 34:6 NASB

Tears can fall during joyous occasions such as a wedding or the birth of a child, as well as when painful things—like stubbing your toe or having a tooth extracted—occur. Then again, tears can be prompted by sadness such as going through a divorce or losing a loved one.

Shedding tears is nothing to be ashamed of. In fact, crying is evidence that you are human and that you have feelings. The important thing is having someone close by who understands your tears.

Christ Jesus cried at the report of the death of Lazarus. His tears may have been an expression of sadness at the death of His friend, or they could have represented His joy in knowing Lazarus would soon be brought back to life. He may also have cried over the unbelief or lack of faith that was evident in those around Him.

So, go ahead and cry. Cry when you are happy. Let the tears fall when you are sad.

God has promised to be with you through everything you face.

I can pray the breath prayer, *Hear my cry, Lord,* when—

- my family needs help.

- I am feeling alone.

- I lose a loved one.

- there is trouble all around.

- someone is disrespectful to me.

- I am praying for others.

Hear my cry, Lord.

DRAW ME TO YOUR HEALING PRESENCE, JESUS.

I am the Lord Who heals you.

EXODUS 15:26 AMP

Medicines have become a constant part of television advertisement. But, if you notice, their side effects seem to be almost as bad as the sickness the medicine is designed to aid.

Do you accept that the hay fever or flu that attacks you every season is the norm, just because they are so prevalent? Do you expect your children to get those "childhood diseases" because everyone says "that's life"?

God promised the Israelites, His *chosen* people through the lineage of Abraham, that He would remove all sickness from them (Exodus 23:25 NASB). Christ Jesus said in John 15:16 that He *chose* you. So why not believe and receive that healing promise for you and your family?

Psalm 91:5-6 NIV says not to fear the pestilence or plague. 1 Peter 2:24 NIV says that you have been healed by Jesus' wounds.

Thank God for physicians and respect their knowledge and skill. Thank God for medicines that bring relief. But believe God's Word for your family's healing and protection.

I can pray the breath prayer, *Draw me you Your healing presence, Jesus,* when—

- I am sick.

- my family is sick.

- I am exposed to something contagious.

- I pray for others to be healed.

- a person is given no hope of recovery.

- those who are sick have lost all hope.

Draw me to Your healing presence, Jesus.

Additional copies of this and other
titles from Honor Books are available
from your local bookseller.

Breath Prayers
Breath Prayers for Mothers
Breath Prayers for Women

If you have enjoyed this book,
or if it has had an impact on your life,
we would like to hear from you.

Please contact us at:

HONOR BOOKS
Cook Communications Ministries, Dept. 201
4050 Lee Vance View
Colorado Springs, CO 80918
Or visit our Web site:
www.cookministries.com

HONOR ⊞ BOOKS